What do I always say?
Anyone can cook.

Chef Gusteau, Ratatouille

*Dedicated to my
Great Grandma & Great Grandad*

*Who both continue to provide us all with a
wealth of inspiration*

Oleander Press
16 Orchard Street
Cambridge
CB1 1JT

www.oleanderpress.com

© James Archer
All rights reserved.

This edition published: 2012

No part of this publication may be reproduced, stored in a retrieval system, or transmitted, in any form or by any means without prior permission in writing of the publisher, nor be otherwise circulated in any form of binding or cover other than in which it is published and without a similar condition including this condition being imposed on the subsequent purchaser.

A CIP catalogue record for the book is available from the British Library.

ISBN: 9780900891847

Design, typeset and photography by James Archer
james@coastlinegraphics.co.uk

Printed by Coastline Graphics on sustainably sourced paper

www.olivers-kitchen.co.uk   Twitter: @ollieskitchen   www.facebook.com/oliverskitchen

OLIVER'S KITCHEN

YEAR 1

Written by
James Archer

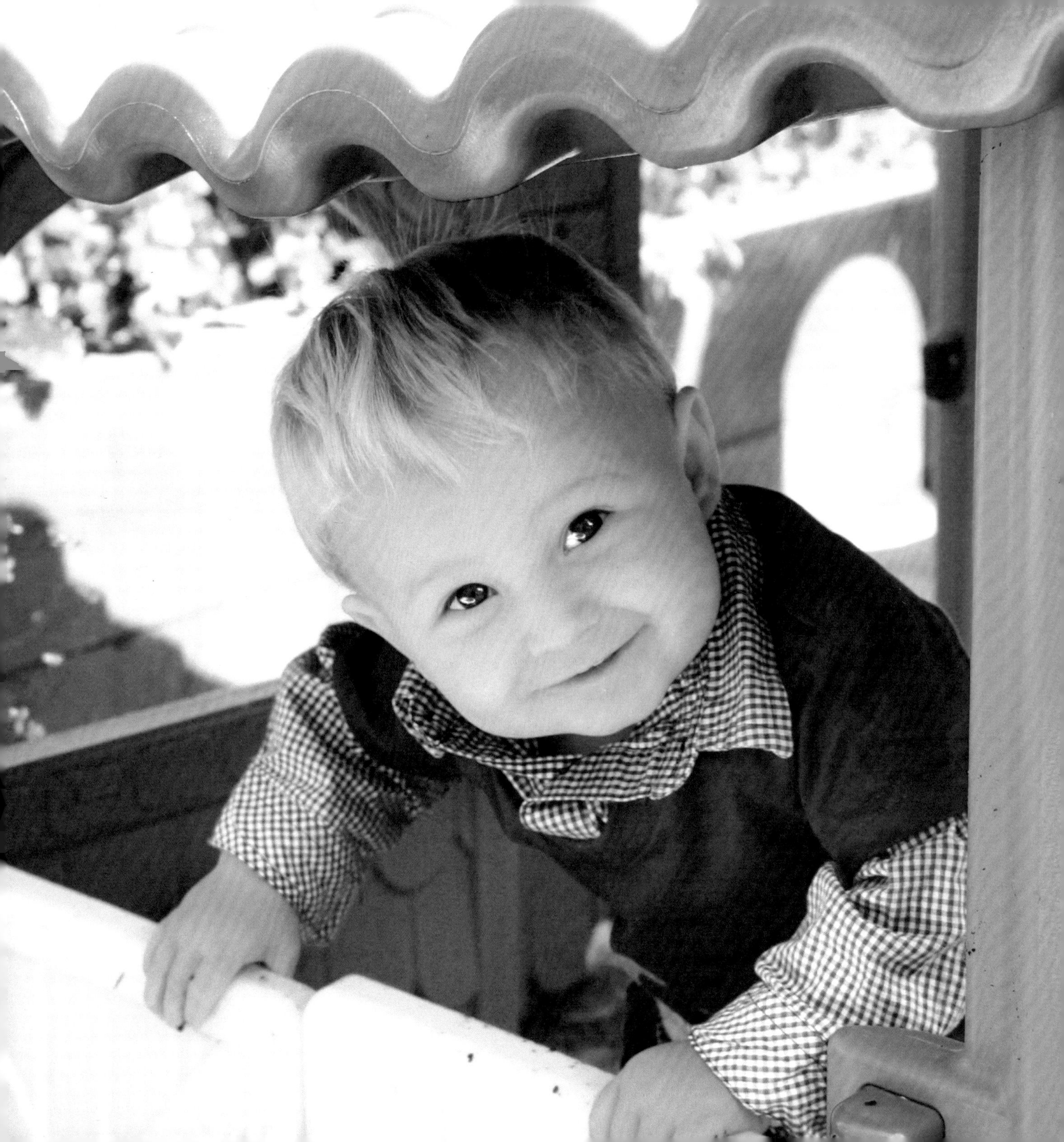

Contents

07 INTRODUCTION

09 THE BEGINNING OF OLLIE'S JOURNEY

10 SPRING
- A tasty Carrot Cake
- Sunday morning Banana Pancakes
- Mia's favourite Fairy Cakes
- Royal Scones with jam & clotted cream
- Slow cooked Braised Salmon

28 SUMMER
- Yummy Chocolate Chip Cookies
- Star Cookies
- Italian Meatballs & Spaghetti
- Build your own Herb Garden
- Delicious French Omelette

46 AUTUMN
- Country Fresh Blueberry Muffins
- Traditional Cornish Pasties
- Spooky Spider Halloween Cake
- Classic Victoria Sponge
- Ollie's First Sloe Gin

66 WINTER
- Home-made Sausage Rolls
- Tomato Soup & Bread Rolls
- Festive Mince Pies
- Christmassy Cup Cakes
- Lemon & Herb Chicken on Couscous

a good cook
never lacks friends

INTRODUCTION

Welcome to Oliver's Kitchen

This book is a celebration of life and cooking. Now despite popular belief, I am not a trained chef. I do however enjoy cooking and, as you will discover, this book is about enjoying the cooking experience as much as the tasty food. So I invite you to take a look at the world through the eyes of a one year old as we embark on a year long journey through the seasons, cooking as we go!

The art of cooking is like painting, it is subjective and can be very messy but that's half the fun, so use your imagination, change things, add ingredients, see what works and if it goes wrong then at least you have enjoyed the process!

There are twenty recipes in this book, cooked throughout the year giving you a brief insight into the world of cooking and just how enjoyable it can be. For best results always try and do your part responsibly for the environment. Always use free range eggs and other ingredients sourced from sustainable, higher welfare origins. If possible, grow your own vegetables and herbs, which can be an enjoyable and rewarding experience in itself. We have four beautiful chickens laying delicious eggs throughout the year, a small vegetable patch and a herb garden. All are easy to maintain and provide valuable fresh produce for our kitchen.

This book also touches on a more serious subject - Childhood Stroke. I had a stroke when I was born but fortunately so far I am doing great. I would, however, like to try and raise people's awareness of childhood strokes and hopefully give other people affected some guidance as to where they can find information and support if they need it. On my website, www.olivers-kitchen.co.uk you will find information and links to valuable support and support groups.

When I started out in the kitchen I had no idea what was to follow so grab your wooden spoons and see where your journey takes you.

Happy cooking everyone!

Olie

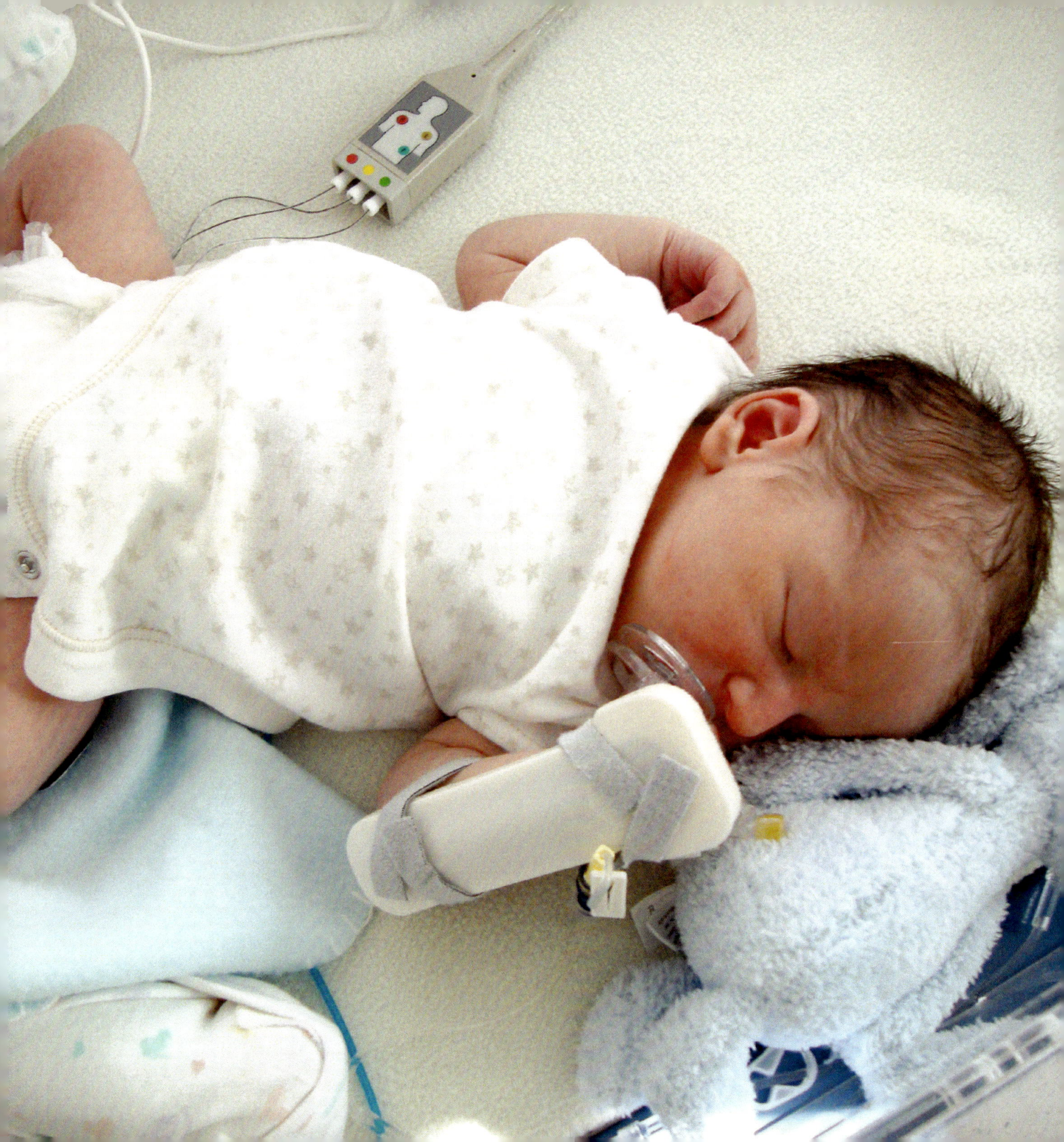

Oliver James Archer
From a troublesome start to a star in the kitchen

- 50% of mummy
- 50% of daddy
- 9 months in a warm cosy place
- 1 stroke during labour
- 7 days of special care in the Neonatal Unit
- 7 nights of prayers
- 1 year of regular hospital visits and consults
- numerous physiotherapy sessions
- a lifetime of love from an amazing big sister
= 1 special little boy

THE BEGINNING OF OLLIE'S JOURNEY

SPRING

- **A tasty Carrot Cake**
- **Sunday morning Banana Pancakes**
- **Mia's favourite Fairy Cakes**
- **Royal Scones with jam and clotted cream**
- **Slow cooked Braised Salmon**

Well spring is here and what a wonderful time of year it is. Everything is fresh and new. A time for new beginnings and fresh starts.

This is where it all began, where we entered the world of cooking. One lazy Sunday afternoon we decided to make a Carrot Cake and document the process in pictures. I then got Dad onto making a blog to show the world our results. We proceeded to make some other tasty recipes including our ultimate breakfast treat - Banana Pancakes and some lovely Scones to celebrate William and Kate's Royal Wedding.

During these early months of the year we enjoy all of the household's birthdays so baking has become quite a theme for this time of year, perfect for experimenting and barely a week went past without there being some sort of cake in the house!

In April I celebrated my first birthday. The last year was a particularly difficult one for us all with various hospital consults, physiotherapy and home visits to check on my progress month by month. But, with the help of my parents and big sister, I have learned to crawl, walk and develop incredibly well and luckily so far I have met all the milestones that seemed so unlikely all those months ago. We took each day as it came and tried not to think too much about the long term, making sure we enjoyed each passing week as much as possible. At the time, the year seemed to pass incredibly slowly but looking back now it has gone in the blink of an eye, proving just how important it is to enjoy these early stages and not let the worry and anxiety overwhelm it.

In May we visited the hospital and met with Dr. Evans like we have many times before, the difference this time however, was that he was so happy with my progress that he signed me off from any future planned hospital visits! This was incredible news and we were all so pleased. It was like a fresh start for us all.

So enjoy these recipes and look forward to the year ahead!

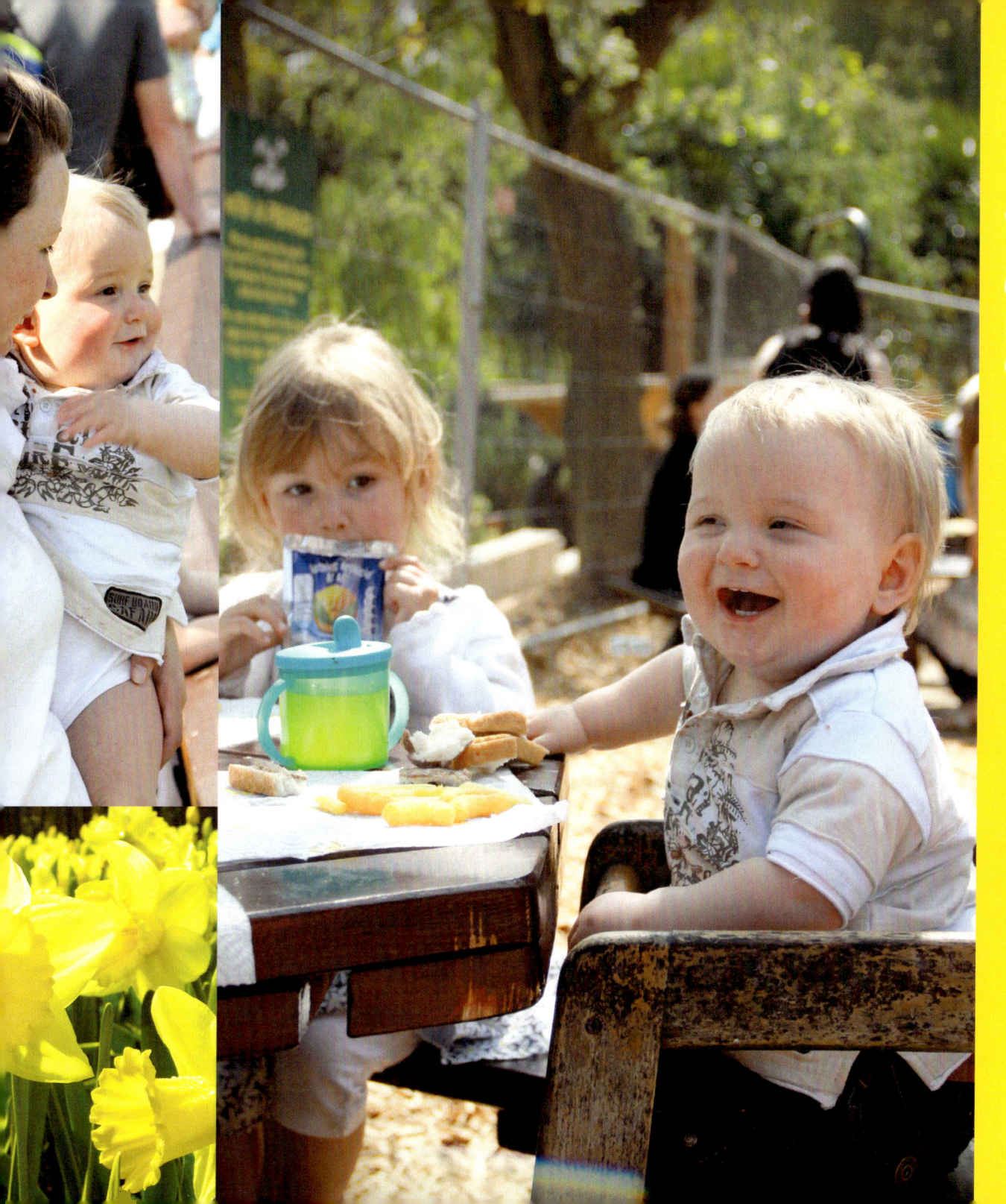

SPRING

Carrot Cake
With a tasty lime mascarpone icing

- 250g butter
- 5 free range eggs
- 250g light brown soft sugar
- juice and zesty bits of 2 little oranges
- 170g self-raising flour
- 1 tsp baking powder
- 100g ground almonds
- 100g chopped walnuts
- 1 tsp ground cinnamon
- 1 tsp of ground ginger
- a pinch of ground nutmeg
- 3 large carrots, grated

for the icing: • 100g mascarpone cheese • 220g cream cheese • 85g icing sugar • 2 limes

1. Firstly, preheat the oven to 180°C and most importantly, clean your work surfaces.

2. Next, beat 250g of butter and 250g of light brown sugar together in a bowl, if it gets too hard then get the nearest big person to help.

3. Next, select 5 of your best free-range eggs. If you're as big as me you can try and crack them with your teeth! If not, just beat in the 5 egg yolks one by one.

4. Next add the zest and juice of 1 orange. Or 2 if you only have baby oranges.

AN AMAZINGLY TASTY CARROT CAKE

13

AN AMAZINGLY TASTY CARROT CAKE

5. Mix together 170g of self-raising flour with a heaped teaspoon of baking powder. It's always best to taste the flour by the way!

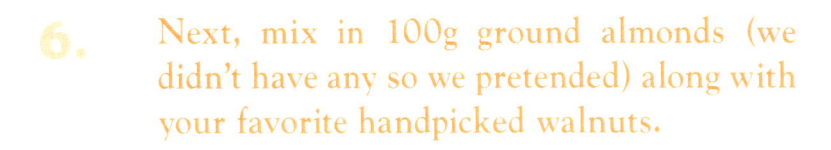

6. Next, mix in 100g ground almonds (we didn't have any so we pretended) along with your favorite handpicked walnuts.

7. Give it a good old mix!

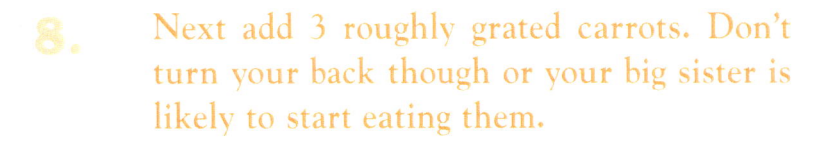

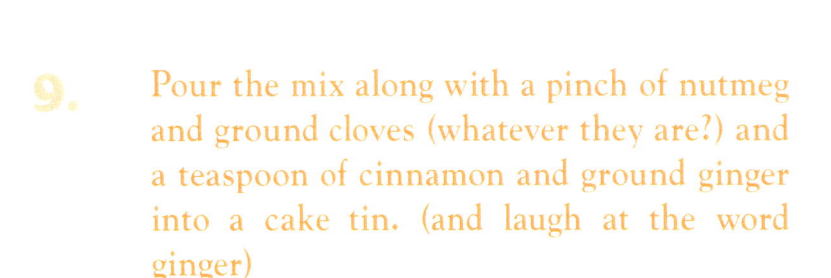

8. Next add 3 roughly grated carrots. Don't turn your back though or your big sister is likely to start eating them.

9. Pour the mix along with a pinch of nutmeg and ground cloves (whatever they are?) and a teaspoon of cinnamon and ground ginger into a cake tin. (and laugh at the word ginger)

10. Place in the preheated oven for 50 minutes and relax for a while, maybe time for a beer?

11. Ok just kidding, maybe time for some juice!

12. Right, now you need to mix 100g of mascarpone cheese, 220g full fat cream cheese, 85g icing sugar and the zest of 2 limes together and spread onto the cake, adding any remaining walnut pieces.

13. All done! Grab a spoon and...... nom nom nom

Banana Pancakes
Pretend like it's the weekend!

- 3 free range eggs
- 115g plain flour
- 1 heaped tsp baking powder
- 140ml milk
- a pinch of salt
- 2 knobs of butter
- 3 tbsp caster sugar
- 4 big old bananas
- vanilla ice cream, cream and chocolate sauce, to serve

1. First, you will need 3 eggs. You're going to need to separate the yolks and the whites. So bang 'em really hard!

2. Combine 115g plain flour, 1 heaped teaspoon of baking powder and 140ml of milk with the egg yolks.

3. Add the egg whites then mix it all up until it forms a smooth, thick batter

4. Then you need a frying pan and some oil, put it on the hob and get it real hot! (Get the bigger people to do this bit!)

5. Whilst one of the big people are frying and tossing the pancakes, get a banana and start slicing it up (it would have been much easier if they would let me have a knife!)

SUNDAY MORNING BANANA PANCAKES

6. Then get your freshly cooked pancake, plop a dollop of ice cream in there along with some slices of banana, some cream and some chocolate sauce. Wrap the little fella up and finish with a squeeze of lemon......
Nom Nom Nom

Mia's Fairycakes
Because they're her favourite!

- 4 fresh free range eggs
- 225g caster sugar
- 225g unsalted butter
- 225g self-rasing flour
- a few squeezes of lemon juice
- icing to decorate

Firstly grab some eggs (obviously free range as you've got to look after your chickens), 4 should do it along with a hula hoop to snack on.

Then you need 225g of caster sugar, 225g of unsalted butter and 225g of self-raising flour.

Then put your (ridiculously happy) sister to work mixing it all up. Don't worry – she seems to be enjoying it! Oh and also add some lemon juice.

Now check it to make sure she did it right!

MIA'S FAVOURITE - FAIRYCAKES!

19

MIA'S FAVOURITE – FAIRYCAKES!

Then you need to get your mixture into the little paper fairy cake holder things.

Pop them in the oven (preheated to 180°c) for about 15 mins. Then prepare some icing and cover the tops of your little cakes. (we made our icing earlier!)

and................Nom Nom Nom!

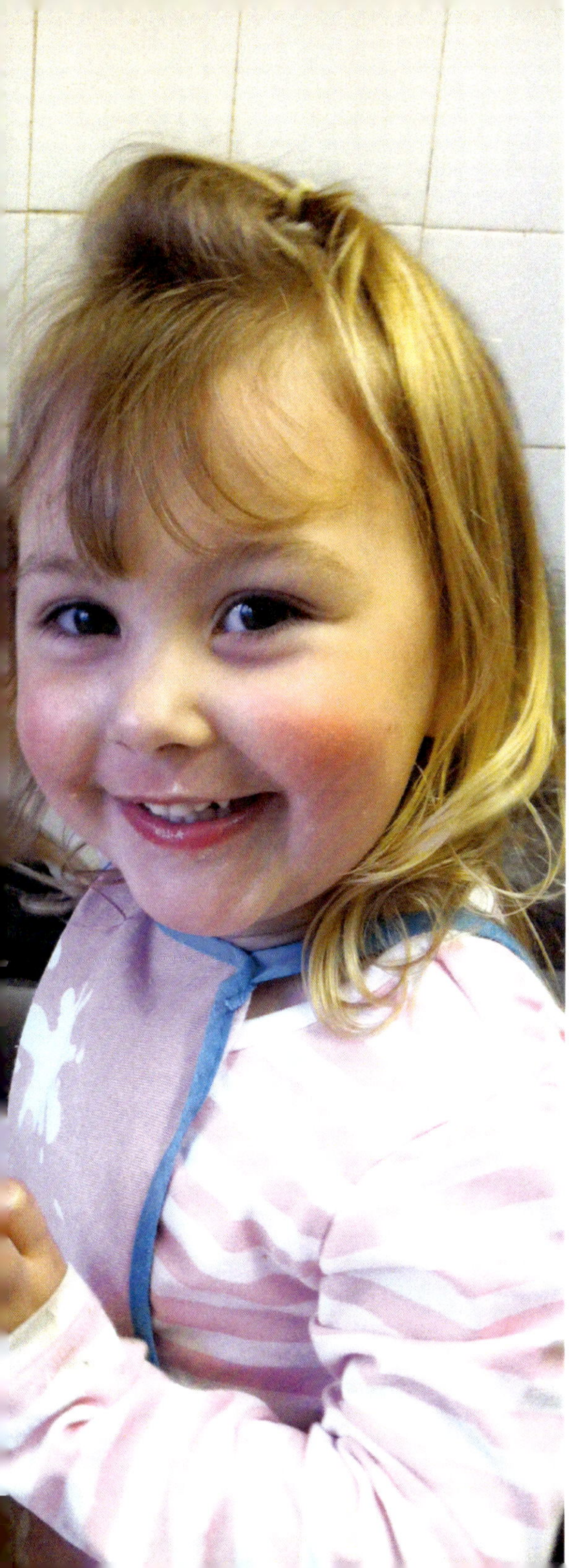

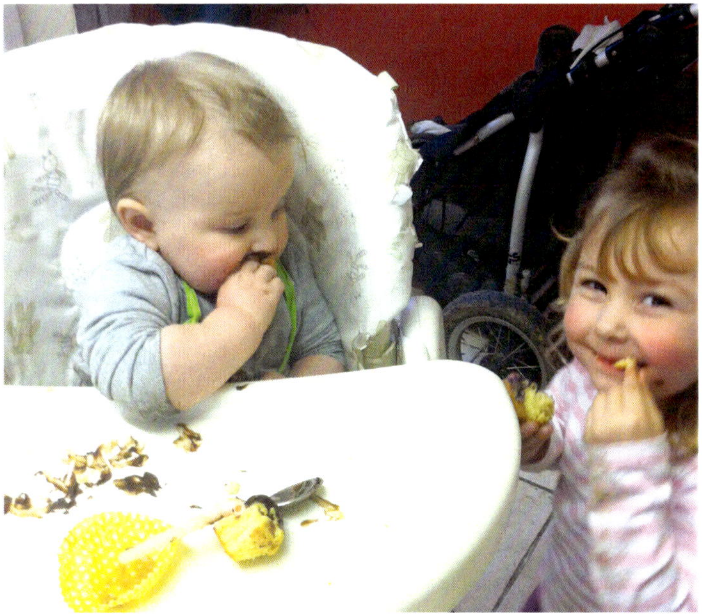

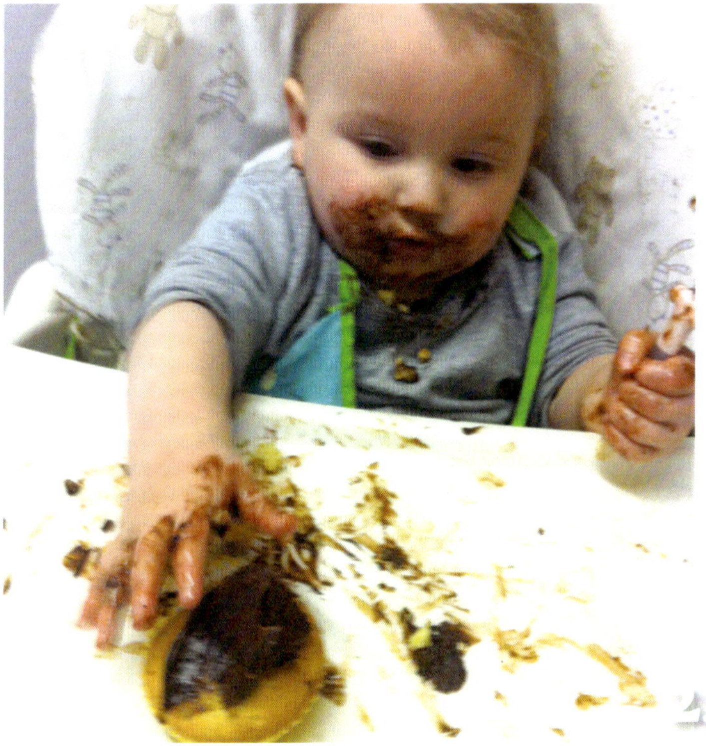

Royal Scones
With jam and clotted cream

- 225g self-raising flour
- 1 heaped tsp baking powder
- 3 tbsp caster sugar
- a pinch of salt
- 50g butter
- 125ml milk
- 1 tsp vanilla extract
- a beaten free range egg to glaze
- strawberry jam and clotted cream to serve

1. Mum made some delicious scones to munch on whilst we celebrated the Royal Wedding and I liked them so much I stole her recipe!

   Firstly you need to mix 225g of self raising flour with a pinch of salt, 3 tablespoons of caster sugar and 1 teaspoon of baking powder, so get the old food blender out.

2. Then add 50g of butter and mix until it becomes like breadcrumbs.

3. Next heat 125ml of milk and the vanilla extract in the microwave for 30 seconds. Add this to the dry mixture and knead into a nice flattish shape about 4cm thick.

4. Then you need to cut out the shapes of your scones, this is the fun bit.

ROYAL SCONES WITH JAM AND CREAM!

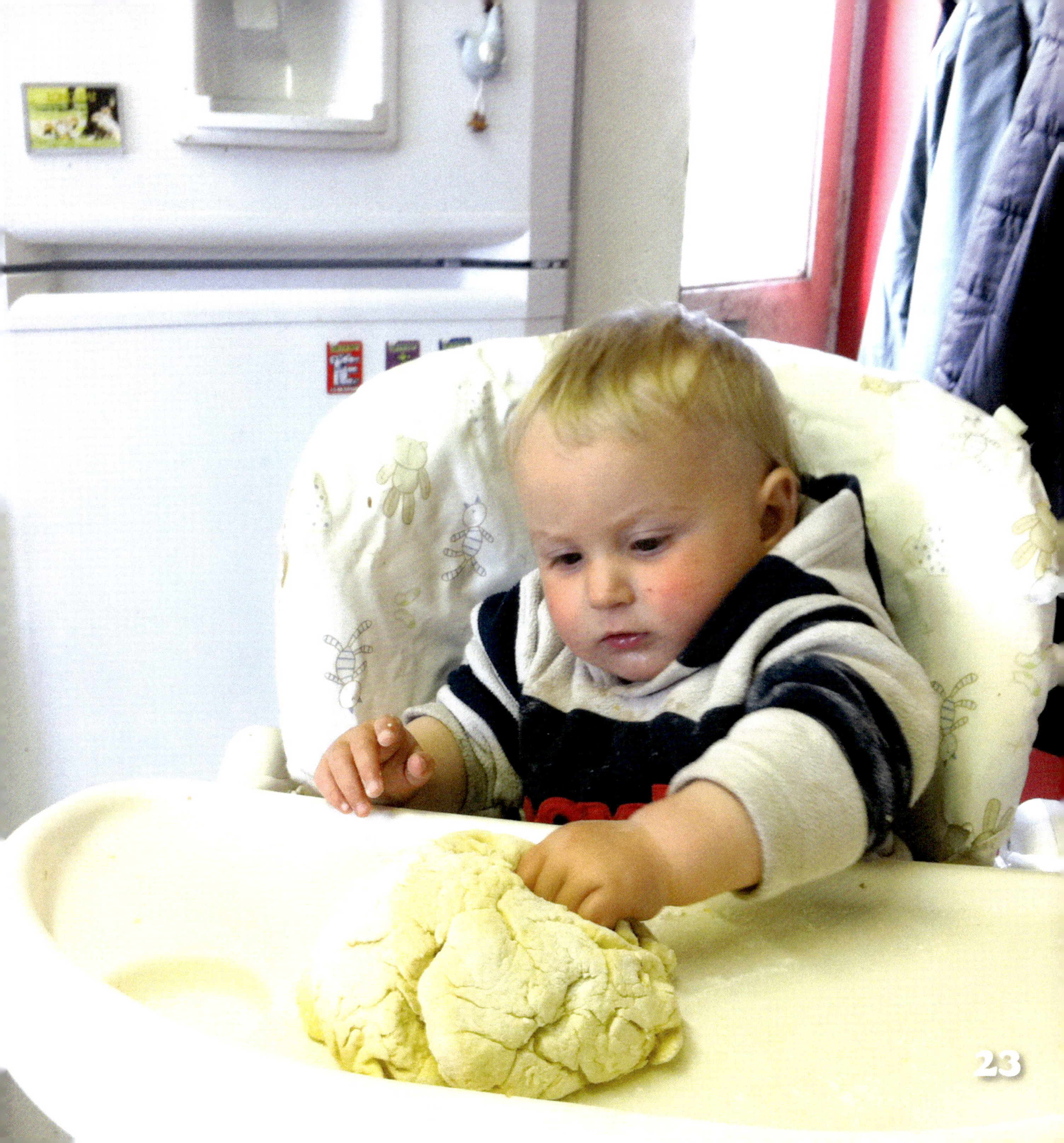

ROYAL SCONES WITH JAM AND CREAM!

5. Now brush on some beaten egg and place on a tray and into the oven (at 180°c) for 12 minutes. Make sure you set your chicken egg timer! You will burn them if you don't!

6. When the little chicken rings take your scones out of the oven and let them cool for a few minutes.

7. Get a big person to cut them all in half and then it's time to fill with clotted cream and strawberry jam!

8. and then it's a very royal nom nom nom!

25

Slow Cooked Braised Salmon
A beautiful dish made easy in the slow cooker!

- 2 large carrots, peeled and cubed
- 2 large onions, peeled and chopped
- 1 medium sweet potato
- 15 baby new potatoes, cut in half
- 100g frozen peas
- 100g green beans, chopped
- 6 tbsp olive oil
- 1 vegetable stock cube
- 4 tbsp soy sauce
- 4 tbsp chopped fresh tarragon
- 300g salmon, skinned and cubed
- 200g crème fraîche
- 4 tbsp chopped fresh chives
- sprinkle of brown sugar

1. Right well it's Mother's Day and we are cooking her some nice Braised Salmon in the slow cooker. For this recipe you will need a few additional bits and bobs, mainly a slow cooker and a monster.

2. You will now need 2 or 3 carrots, a couple of onions, a hand full of potatoes and a few chocolate buttons to snack on.

3. You will then need to cut them all up, luckily I have got pretty good at doing this with a silly plastic knife…

4. Now show your monster how clever you are.

5. Now get the funny old soy sauce out and add a few spoonfuls along with all your chopped veg to the ceramic bowl of the slow cooker and heat it on the hob, add some olive oil, vegetable stock and a sprinkle of brown sugar and let it heat up.

6. Give it a good old stir and add a few seasonal green vegetables. This can now be put on the slow cooker on a low heat setting for about 4 hours after which you add the salmon and tarragon and cook on high for 40 mins. While it's cooking itself we are all off out to enjoy Mother's Day safe in the knowledge our dinner will be ready when we get back! Serve with crème fraîche and chopped chives

SUMMER

- **Yummy Chocolate Chip Cookies**
- **Italian Meatballs & Spaghetti**
- **Star Cookies**
- **Build your own Herb Garden**
- **Delicious French Omelette**

It's summertime! The sun is out and it's the season to be outdoors so nice quick recipes for the kitchen are in order. In this chapter we make some nice cookies to snack on, Mia gets busy building me a fantastic herb garden and we jet off to France to make some nice summer lunch-time omelettes.

This time of year is a particular favourite for the dogs, long evening walks, trips to the dog beach and lazy days on the decking are in abundance. We certainly try and make the most of the later evenings!

I experienced my first flight in an airplane this summer when we flew out to visit my Great Grandparents in France. They are fantastic and made us feel very welcome, we really enjoyed their swimming pool in particular! Whilst there we continued with our culinary adventure cooking some delicious omelettes which we served with some fresh salad from the neighbour's vegetable garden.

During these months my health and development have progressed as normal and we are all feeling really positive about life! The only negative when it comes to health was my dose of chickenpox that unfortunately showed itself on the first day of our summer holiday, sending us home to re-book a few weeks later! Chickenpox is not fun! As Daddy still has not had it - he thinks he has some sort of magical immunity!

Well, go on and enjoy the summer and don't forget to share any cooking experiences you have on our website or Facebook page.

SUMMER

29

Chocolate Chip Cookies
Just because it's always cookie time!

- 2 large free range eggs
- 350g plain flour
- 1 tspn baking powder
- 175g caster sugar
- 1 tsp salt
- 225g butter
- 175g brown sugar
- a dash of vanilla extract
- chunks of chocolate

1. First preheat the oven to 190c. Then combine 350g of flour with 1 tsp baking powder and 1 tsp salt.

2. Then measure out 175g of caster sugar with 225g of butter, 175g brown sugar, and a little vanilla extract on the scales.

3. Beat in the eggs and gradually add the flour. Best taste a little to make sure it is good.

4. Then add the chocolate! (left over easter eggs are perfect!) Once it's all mixed together, roll it out and cut out the cookie shapes.

BIG YUMMY CHOCOLATE CHIP COOKIES!

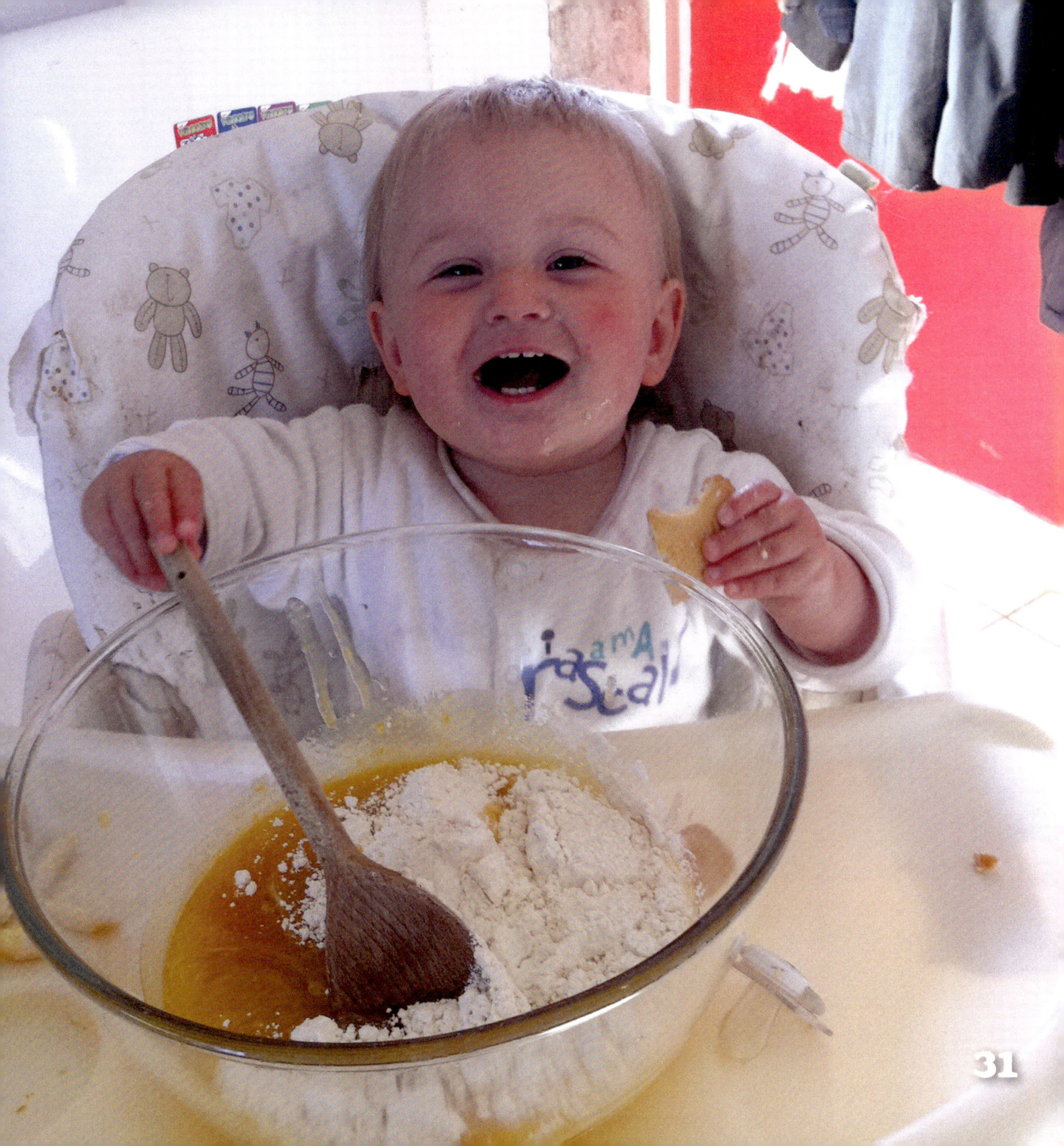
i am A
rascal

BIG YUMMY CHOCOLATE CHIP COOKIES!

5. Place your cookies on a baking tray and bake for 10 minutes. Oh and make sure you set your chicken timer.

6. Then sit back and take a look at how good they look! ...Mmmmmm

33

Tasty Italian Meatballs
A classic dish from the country shaped like a boot!

- a few fresh rosemary twigs
- 12 cream crackers
- 2 heaped tsp Dijon mustard
- 500g good-quality minced beef
- 1 heaped tbsp dried oregano
- 1 lovely large fresh egg
- sea salt & freshly ground black pepper
- olive oil
- a bunch of fresh basil
- 1 onion
- 2 cloves of garlic
- ½ a fresh red chilli or sweet pepper
- 2 tins of chopped tomatoes
- 2 tbsp balsamic vinegar
- 400g dried spaghetti
- parmesan cheese to serve
- 2 tsp pesto

1. This is a fun recipe, firstly smash up the cream crackers into tiny pieces!

2. Next strip the leaves from 4 twigs of rosemary and add to the crackers along with 1 heaped tablespoon of oregano, 500g minced meat, 2 heaped teaspoons of Dijon Mustard and an egg.

3. If you're smart, get some foolish big person to roll out the meatballs while you have a well deserved power nap. Apparently you want to divide the mixture into 4 balls then divide those into a further 6 to make 24(ish). Add some seasoning and olive oil and put them to one side.

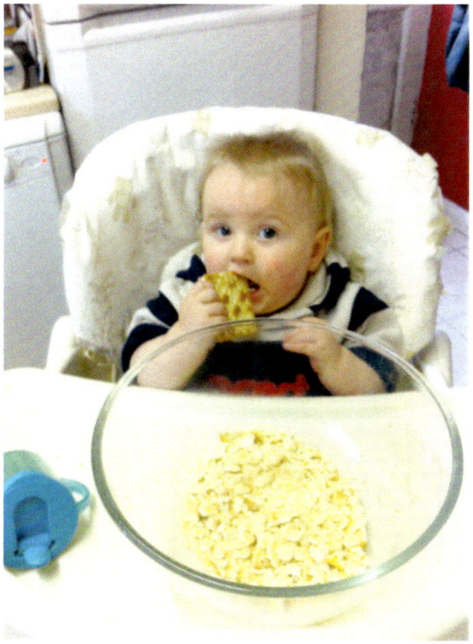

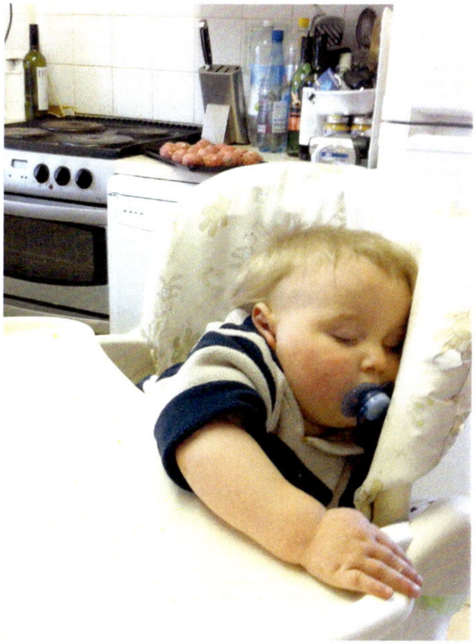

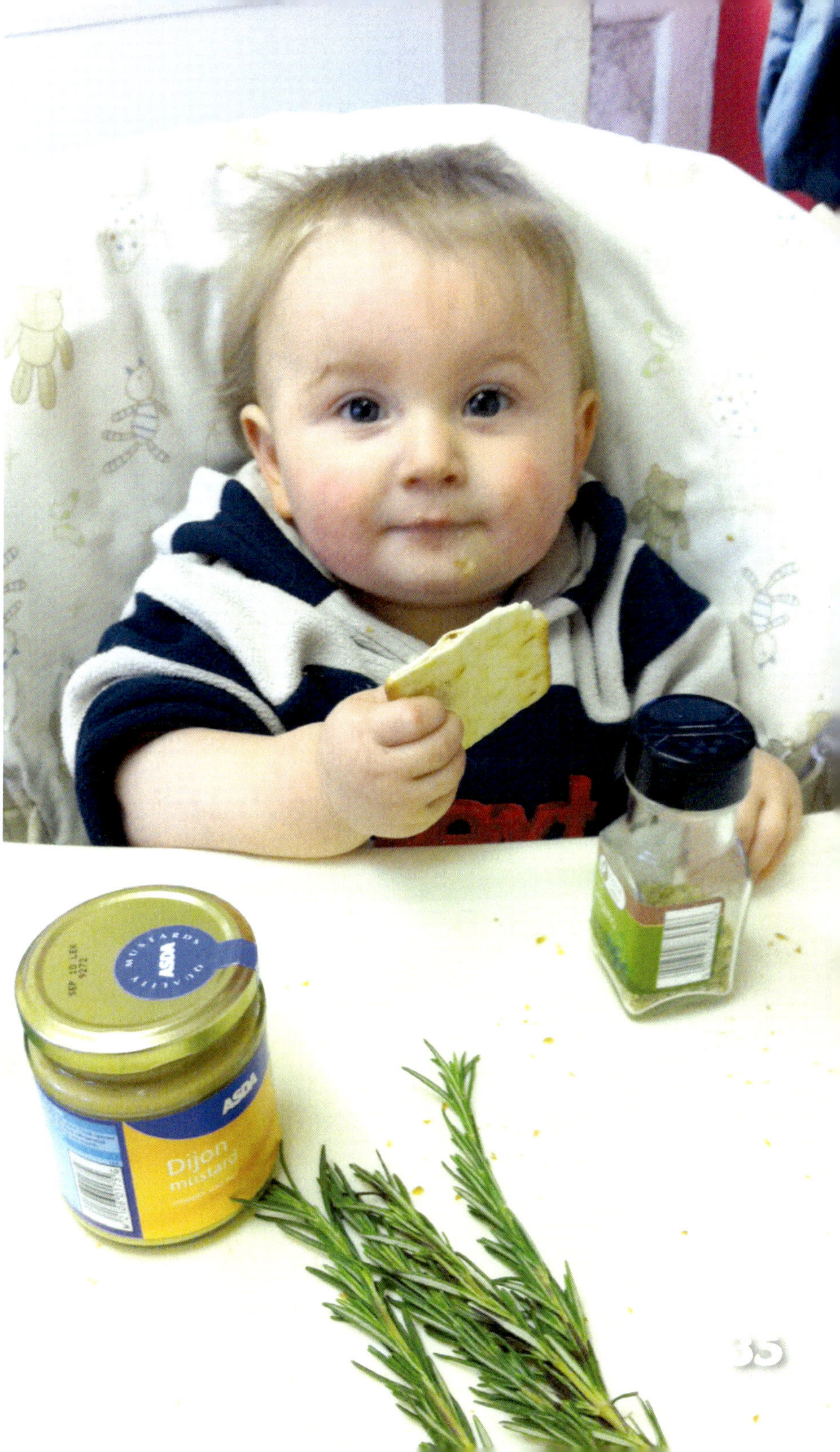
ASDA
ASDA
Dijon mustard

TASTY ITALIAN MEATBALLS

4. Next we need to prepare the sauce, so finely chop 2 cloves of garlic, an onion and half a chilli pepper. As some funny guy only gave me this stupid plastic knife, this proved rather difficult for me! (Good job I had that nap!)

5. Fry these all up in a little olive oil and add some basil leaves, 2 tins of chopped tomatoes and 2 tablespoons of balsamic vinegar. Then fry the meatballs separately in another glug of olive oil and add to the sauce once the meatballs are cooked through. Let it all simmer while you boil a pan of spaghetti.

6. Once the spaghetti is cooked, drain it and mix it with a couple of teaspoons of pesto. Plate up and add some more basil leaves then top it all off with some parmesan cheese!….
Nom Nom Nom!

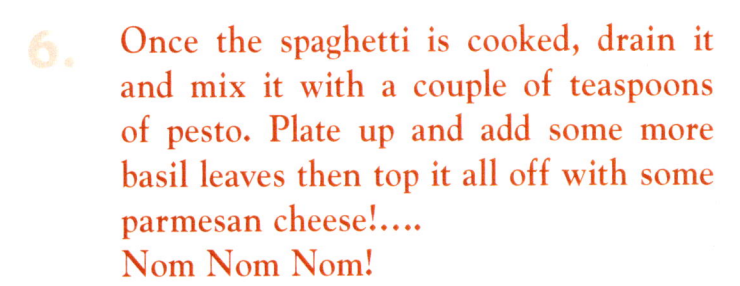

(These can be a little spicy so choose your chillies carefully or replace with sweet peppers!)

37

Star Cookies
Special iced cookies perfect for a mid-day snack!

- 100g butter
- 100g caster sugar
- 1 tsp vanilla extract
- 1 free range egg
- 225g plain flour
- 500g ready to roll white icing
- 1 tbsp strawberry jam
- a handfull of chocolate stars to decorate

Firstly preheat the oven to 180°c and grease a baking tray.

Beat the butter and sugar in a large bowl until soft and fluffy. Add the vanilla extract, 1 tablespoon of flour and the egg. (Be careful not to drop the egg in and splash yourself in the eye! - that would be irritating)

Add the remaining flour and beat again.

Bring the mixture together into a ball using your hands and chill in the fridge for an hour. Have a well deserved rest after all that mixing!

On a slightly floured surface, roll out the dough and cut star shapes from it with a star cutter.

STAR SHAPED ICED COOKIES

39

STAR SHAPED ICED COOKIES

Place on a baking tray and bake for in the oven for 10-12 minutes.

Roll out the icing to a thickness of 0.5cm then use the same star cutter to cut star shapes from it.

Spread a dollop of jam on the cookie and top with the icing star to complete your cookies! I got Mia to do this bit as I quite fancied a nap!

Nom nom nom!

41

Build Your Own Herb Garden
Mia & Ollie build their own herb garden

- some lengths of timber
- a handful of nails
- a bag of compost
- a selection of herb plants

Every good chef needs a good herb garden and as I'm only tiny I thought it only right that I get Mia to make me one…

1. It's quite simple, you just need some wood and a saw

2. Then you need to cut the wood up into lengths, we are making a shallow square box with a base.

3. Then you bang some nails into the lengths of wood to hold them together. You can also nail the base piece of wood in place in the same way, just mind your fingers!

4. Then when all 4 sides are nailed together and the base is on, you can fill it with compost (posh mud)

5. And now you are ready to start planting your herbs, I started with Basil

6. And your done, add as many herbs as will comfortably fit, here we have mint, basil, parsley and lemon balm and we will add some more later. Soon to be ready to use in our next recipe!

Delicious French Omelette
Ollie cooks yummy omelettes whilst on holiday in France

- 3 large free range eggs
- a knob of butter
- 1 tsp finely grated fresh parmesan
- 3 tbsp finely grated Gruyère
- some fresh ham
- a splash of milk

While visiting our Great Grandparents in France we made sure we had time for a bit of cooking! Here is a traditional French omelette recipe that made a lovely lunch!

1. Pick 3 of the best eggs and crack them into a bowl, add a splash of milk and beat them with a fork.

2. Heat a frying pan up to a medium heat and drop one knob of butter into the pan. It should bubble and sizzle. Season the eggs with the Parmesan and a little salt and pepper, and pour into the pan.

3. This bit can be a bit tricky so we let Mum do this part. Let the eggs bubble slightly for a couple of seconds, then take a wooden spoon and gently draw the mixture in from the sides of the pan a few times, so it gathers in folds in the centre. Repeat this to make sure you cook all of the egg. With the pan flat on the heat, shake it back and forth a few times to settle the mixture. It should slide easily in the pan and look soft and moist on top. Then add the ham and Gruyère to warm for a few seconds.

DELICIOUS OMELETTES COOKED IN FRANCE

4. Slide the omelette out of the pan and fold over.

We had ours with some home-made chips and fresh salad - Nom nom nom.

45

AUTUMN

- **Country Fresh Blueberry Muffins**
- **Traditional Cornish Pasties**
- **Spooky Spider Halloween Cake**
- **Classic Victoria Sponge**
- **Ollie's First Sloe Gin**

Autumn already! This year is flying past too. This is a great time of year, all the leaves changing colour and don't forget Halloween! In this chapter we have recipes for some nice comfort food; some gorgeous blueberry muffins with blueberries fresh from the garden, sloe gin which apparently is delicious although I'm not allowed to try it and a fun spooky spider cake during our Halloween preparations.

Daddy loves this time of year but I think its mainly because him and Mummy both start to get excited about Christmas much earlier than most people!

At the beginning of Autumn we celebrated my Christening. We had an amazing day but I have to say that having cold water poured on your head in a church full of your friends and family may be funny for everyone else but I was not impressed! Thanks to all the family who helped out with the catering, you should find some recipes here inspired by your efforts!

Enjoy this season of change and embrace the new possibilities it creates in the kitchen.

AUTUMN

47

Blueberry Muffins
With freshly picked blueberries from the garden

- 340g plain flour
- 1 tsp baking powder
- 225g caster sugar

- 120g melted butter
- 2 medium free-range eggs, beaten
- 250g natural yoghurt
- a bowl full of freshly picked blueberries

We have a lovely young blueberry bush in our garden and this is the second year that we have been able to pick some of the yummy berries. As they compliment muffins so well it would be rude not to make some!

1. Firstly preheat the oven to 200°C and line a 12-hole muffin tin with some nice little cases.

2. Sift the flour and baking powder into a large bowl and stir in the sugar.

3. In a separate bowl combine the butter with the eggs and yoghurt.

COUNTRY FRESH BLUEBERRY MUFFINS

49

COUNTRY FRESH BLUEBERRY MUFFINS

4. Lightly stir the mixture into the flour, making sure it is all well mixed.

5. Stir in the blueberries then spoon the mixture into the paper cases, filling nearly to the top. Bake them for 25 minutes making sure you set your chicken timer - you have been warned!

Remove from the oven, place on a cooling rack then enjoy!

TRADITIONAL CORNISH PASTIES

Cornish Pasties
A fine traditional pasty fit for a king

- 500g plain flour
- 125g butter, diced
- 125g lard, diced
- 1 tbsp sunflower oil
- 1 onion
- 150g swede
- 150g potato
- 100g carrot
- 350g sirloin steak, cut up small
- 1 fresh free range egg, beaten

1. Get your hands in and rub together the flour, butter and lard until it resembles bread crumbs. Add about 5 tablespoons of ice-cold water and mix into a firm dough. Cover and place in the fridge to chill for about 20 mins.

2. Get a big person to heat the sunflower oil in a pan and cook the onions for about 5 minutes. Tip into a bowl and add the swede, potato and carrot. Season well with salt and ground pepper.

3. Preheat the oven to 200°c. Roll out the pastry and cut out 4 circles around a 20cm plate. Place a quarter of the veg mix on one half of each circle and top with the steak. Brush the edges with egg. Fold the pastry over the filling and crimp the edges with your fingers. Quite tricky this bit, sometimes it's better to ask a big person for some help.

53

TRADITIONAL CORNISH PASTIES

4. Place on baking tray, brush with egg and chill for 15 minutes. Bake for 10 minutes.

5. Reduce the temperature to 180°c and bake for 40 minutes.

6. Remove from the oven and nom nom nom!

Perfect as a midday snack or with some fresh vegetables and gravy for dinner!

55

Spooky Spider Cake
The perfect dessert to celebrate Halloween!

- 250g dark belgium cooking chocolate
- 200g butter
- 200g light brown sugar
- 100ml soured cream
- 2 free range eggs
- 1 tsp vanilla extract
- 200g self-raising flour
- 5 tbsp cocoa powder
- 250g golden icing sugar
- 8 crunchy mint sticks
- 1 mallow tea cake
- x2 writing icing pens in black & white

1. It's a spook time of year so what better to cook than a creepy spider cake! Make sure you are dressed appropriately!

   Preheat the oven to 160°c and grease the base of a 20cm round cake tin.

2. This part is best left to the big people. Over a low heat, melt 200g of chocolate with the butter, brown sugar and 100ml hot water, stirring continuously. Remove and cool for 2-3 minutes.

3. Stir in the soured cream, eggs, and vanilla extract. Sieve together the flour and cocoa powder then whisk into the chocolate mixture.

4. Pour into the cake tin and cook for 50-60 mins. To make sure it is cooked get a big person to stick a skewer in it and see if it comes out clean. Leave to cool and go to town licking the chocolatey bowl!

57

SPOOKY SPIDER HALLOWEEN CAKE

5. Place the icing sugar into a bowl, add some cold water, a little at a time. Mix until the mixture becomes spreadable.

6. Turn your cake over (so the top is flat) and spread a generous amount of the icing on top allowing it to dribble down the sides.

7. Melt the remaining 50g of chocolate then allow it to cool and thicken. Using a disposable piping bag, pipe a spiders web on top of the cake. This is definitely trickier than it looks so get a big person to help you.

8. Place the tea cake in the centre to form the spider's body. Use the icing pens to create the eyes.
Cut the mint sticks and use the melted chocolate as a glue, creating the legs.

There you have a yummy dessert ready for Halloween!

Victoria Sponge
A simple but tasty classic sponge with jam

- 1/2 tsp of oil for greasing
- 170g butter
- 170g caster sugar
- 4 free range eggs
- 170g self-raising flour, sifted
- 3 tbsp raspberry jam
- 1 tsp icing sugar for dusting

1. Firstly preheat the oven to 180°c and grease two cake tins.

2. Cream the butter and sugar together until light and fluffy. Gradually add the eggs, just a little at a time, beating them well between each addition. Maybe ask a slightly bigger person if you get tired.

3. Fold in the flour and add 3 tablespoons of water to bring the mixture to a perfect dripping consistency.

4. Drip the mixture between the 2 tins

5. Bake in the oven for 25 minutes until the cakes are well risen and a nice golden colour. mmmm yum!

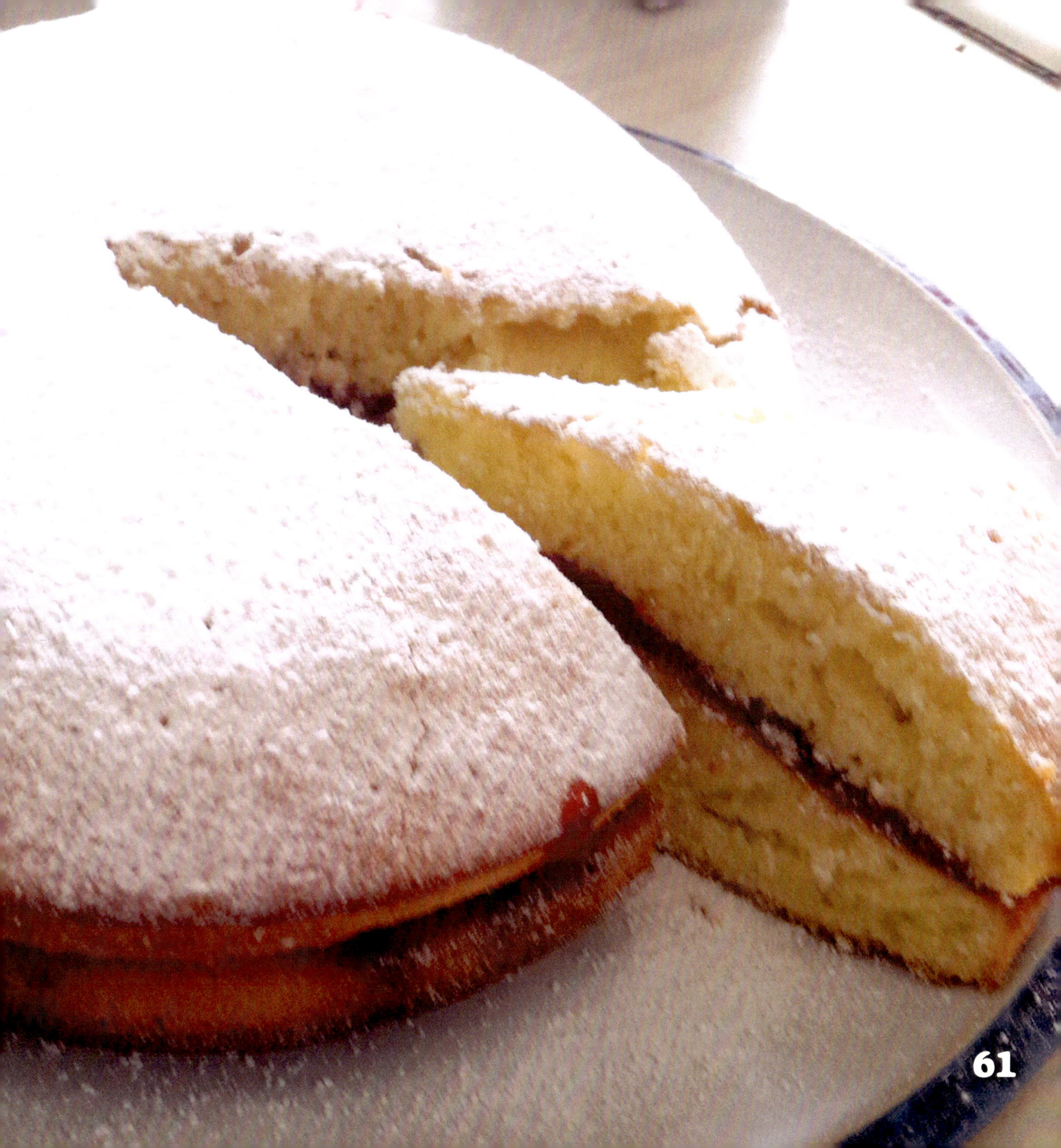

CLASSIC VICTORIA SPONGE CAKE

6. Leave the cakes to cool completely.

7. Spread the jam onto one of the bases then sandwich them both together. Dust the top with icing sugar then… nom nom nom!

(you can name your sponge anything you like by the way, it doesn't have to be Victoria. I named mine Steve.

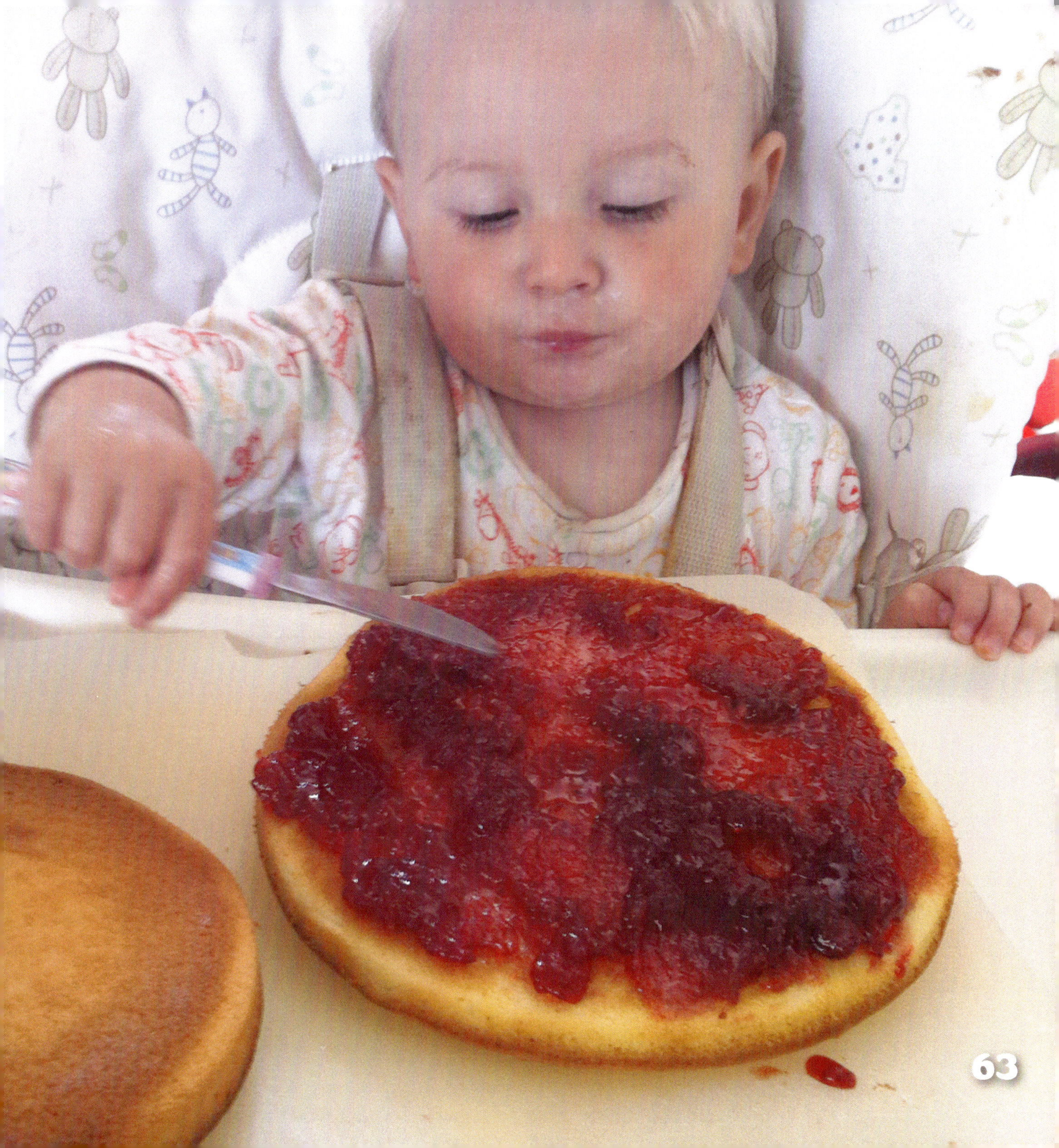

Ollie's 1st Sloe Gin
Baby Ollie makes his first ever batch of sloe gin

- 3 pints of sloes
- 1lb 10oz sugar
- 4 pints of gin

1. Right well after the success of Mia's 1st Sloe Gin, it is now my turn!

   Firstly you need to wrap up warm and head out to find some sloes! They are normally found along hedge rows just out of reach of us little ones, so it is always a good idea to drag one of those bigger people out with you to help.

2. Once you have a few bags full, you need to get them home, light the fire and settle down to the task of pricking them!

   To do this, prick the tough skin of the sloes all over with a clean needle and put in a large sterilised demijohn (glass bottle).

3. Pour in the sugar and the gin, seal tightly and shake well.

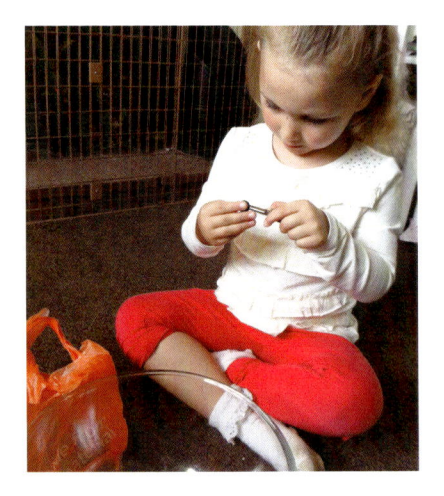

Store in a cool, dark cupboard and shake every other day for a week. Then shake once a week for at least two months.

When it is finally ready, strain the sloe gin through muslin into sterilised bottles.
Then apparently you have to wait 17 years until your old enough to drink!?

WINTER

- **Home-made Sausage Rolls**
- **Tomato Soup & Bread Rolls**
- **Festive Mince Pies**
- **Christmassy Cup Cakes**
- **Lemon & Herb Chicken on Couscous**

Winter is a fantastic time of year for cooking - think soups, cakes and Christmas food! Perfect for experimenting and trying out new recipes. In this chapter we explore these possibilities and cook a tangy tomato soup with some fresh baked bread rolls, some Christmas themed cupcakes, mince pies and some snack food in the form of tasty sausage rolls.

This really is a family time of year and we often have friends and family round for food, whether it be 3 course meals, feasts of nibbles or just some snacks.

There is nothing better than coming in out of the cold to a cosy open fire and a bowl of hot soup, it really puts you in the mood to start the important Christmas preparations which we all enjoy so much! And don't forget the mince pies and carrots for Santa and his reindeer!

So make sure you all enjoy the quieter early part of winter as the Christmas chaos comes around quicker than you think!

As the year draws to an end, so does our journey. We hope you all enjoy your time in the kitchen and make some amazing food. Have a read of the following recipes and as always we would love to hear your feedback, you never know if the response is good we may need to crack on with book two!

Happy cooking

WINTER

67

Home-made Sausage Rolls
Perfect as a snack or for a picnic

- 375g ready rolled puff pastry sheet
- 1 free range egg
- 12 chipolatas
- 1 tsp fennel seeds
- some cheese for grating
- a handful of sesame seeds

1. Firstly get a grown-up to preheat the oven to 220°c and grease a baking tray.

2. Dust a clean surface with the flour and unroll the puff pastry. Slice the pastry in half lengthways, Beat the egg in a little bowl, then use the pastry brush to paint the pastry halves just like you would paint a picture.

3. Line up 6 chipolatas (which I think are just thinner sausages but I'm not sure) on each half of the pastry halves. Bash up 1 teaspoon of fennel seeds and sprinkle over.

4. Finely grate a nice layer of cheese over the sausages.

5. Now, get your big sister to fold the pastry over the sausages and use a fork to crimp the edges together. This should leave you with 2 long sausage rolls which is how I think they should stay!

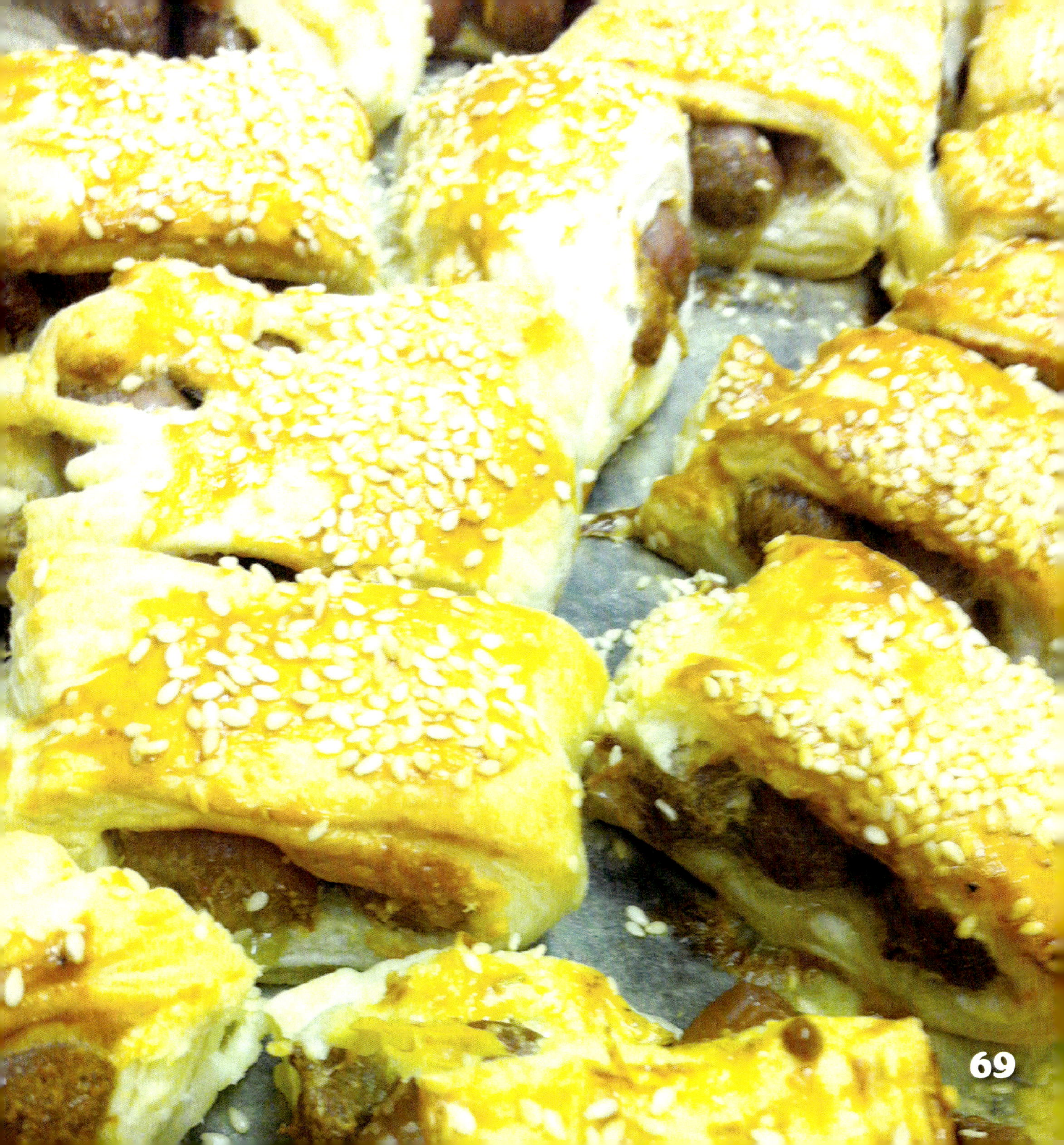

HOME-MADE SAUSAGE ROLLS

Paint them with the rest of the egg and sprinkle over the sesame seeds.

Drizzle some olive oil over a baking tray then slice up the big long sausage rolls (boooooo!) into smaller pieces and place on the tray.

Get one of the big people to put them into the oven for 15 minutes.

They should now be golden brown and ready to be taken out of the oven.

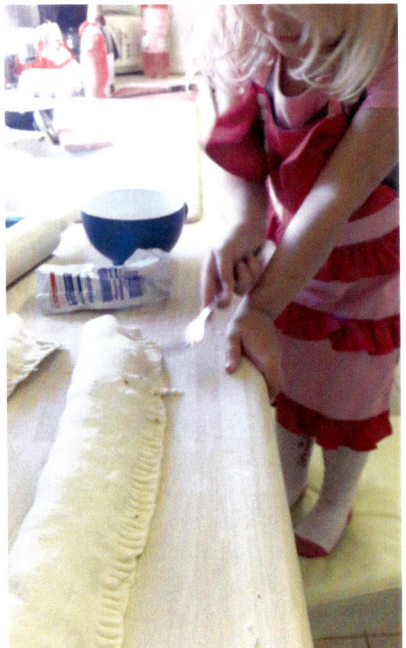

Now you can either pack them up ready for your picnic (the zoo is always a good place to go, even in winter) or pop them on a plate and enjoy as part of a feast!

Tomato Soup & Bread Rolls
A fresh alternative to the tinned favourite!

- 2kg fresh tomatoes
- 2 carrots
- some fresh basil
- 2 tbsp brown sugar (optional)
- 5 tbsp single cream
- salt and pepper

For the bread:
- 275ml water
- 450g strong white bread flour
- 1.5 tbsp dried milk powder
- 1.5 tsp salt
- 2 tsp caster sugar
- 25g butter
- 1.5 tsp easy blend dried yeast

1. Fire the old oven up to 180°c

2. Right, now you need to add the tomatoes, carrots and some basil to the blender and give it a good blast. You should probably get a grown up for this bit. (just in case the lid isn't on properly)

3. Once it is nice and smooth, move it into a saucepan and leave on a low heat for 20 mins (definitely get a grown up for this bit!)

4. Right, now earlier on we used our breadmaker to make some bread dough. The actual process may differ between breadmakers but the basics are to add all the ingredients listed above and wait for it to do it's magic!

5. When the dough is ready, it will need rolling out and splitting into 10 pieces. Leave them to rise for an hour, brush with milk or egg and sprinkle with sesame seeds.
Place in the oven for 10-15 mins

6. While the bread is cooking, turn up the heat on the soup and add the optional brown sugar and the cream. Season well and it's ready to serve with your fresh warm bread rolls!

Festive Mince Pies

There is nothing better in winter than the aroma of warm mince pies

- 175g plain flour
- 100g unsalted butter
- 1 medium egg yolk, beaten
- 350g mincemeat
- icing sugar for dusting

1. Firstly we need to make some pastry. So rub the flour and butter together in a bowl. Make a little well in the centre of the dough and add the egg yolk. Kind of like making a sand castle!

2. Then add 1 tablespoon cold water and work it into the dough, adding more if necessary. Knead gently until smooth then wrap in cling film and chill in the fridge for 15 minutes.

3. Preheat the oven to 200°c.

4. On a floured surface, roll out the pastry to a thickness of about 0.5cm. Using a 7cm round cutter, stamp out 12 circles and line a 12 hole tart tin with them.

5. Spoon a generous teaspoon of mincemeat into each case. Roll out the remaining dough and cut out some nice holly leaves for the tops.

6. Bake in the oven for 10 minutes then reduce the oven temperature to 180°c and bake for a further 8-10 minutes, until golden brown. Cool on a rack, dust with the icing sugar then Nom nom nom!

Christmassy Mini Cup Cakes
The perfect little treat for the best time of the year!

- 3 clementines (baby oranges)
- 90g caster sugar
- 90g butter
- 2 free range eggs
- 90g self-raising flour

For the icing:
- 175g icing sugar
- 1½ tbsp warm water
- some roll out icing for decoration
- red and green food colouring

1. Heat the oven up to 190°c, then put a paper case into each hole of a cake tray.

2. Grate the zest from the clementines or baby oranges. Then beat it in a bowl with the sugar and butter. Add the eggs and flour and beat until well mixed

3. Use a teaspoon to divide the mixture between the cases then bake for 15 minutes until firm and risen. Then squeeze the juice from the little oranges over the cakes while they are still warm.

4. Put the cakes on a wire rack and leave to cool.

5. Sift the icing sugar into a bowl then mix it with the warm water. Spread onto each of the cakes.

6. Take a small amount of the roll out icing and dye it red with the red food colouring for the berries. Do the same with a larger piece of icing but this time make it green for the leaves.

7. Use a holly shaped cutter and decorate your little cakes with some festive holly!

Lemon & Herb Chicken
Lemon, herb and honey flavoured chicken on couscous

- 9 chicken drumsticks
- lemon juice and honey
- a few splashes of olive oil
- a pinch of thyme
- couscous
- half an onion, chopped finely
- a few sticks of celery
- some rough chopped cucumber
- a handful of mixed lettuce leaves
- prepared chicken stock

1. Mix some honey, thyme and fresh lemon juice in a little bowl.

2. Lay some chicken drumsticks in an oven tray and grate some lemon zest, then spread the honey/lemon mixture over the chicken.

3. Cook the chicken in a preheated oven at 180°c for about 20 minutes checking that it is cooked thoroughly throughout. As usual this is a grown up job so take some time to examine the herb pots!

4. Whilst the chicken is cooking lets start making the couscous. For this we need to combine 1 part couscous with 1.5 parts hot chicken stock. We prepared our own chicken stock from a chicken we cooked earlier in the week - a great way of getting the most out of each meal!

5. Let the couscous stand for 5 minutes then give it a good stir. The chicken should now be cooked so place the couscous onto a bed of salad with the drumsticks laying on top - ready for the table!

Thanks

Well that's it, I hope you have enjoyed our little adventure as much as we have!

There are so many wonderful people that I would like to thank. Unfortunately there is not room to mention you all so if your name is not here, I'm deeply sorry and well, thank you!

To my amazing Mummy who has loved, cared and looked after me my whole life, you are quite simply the best Mummy! To my Daddy for the late nights typing, holding the camera and voicing my thoughts! To Mia, you have already taught me so much and are a fantastic big sister. And to my two dogs, Gemma and Megan for being my four legged best friends and protectors!

To the rest of my incredible family and friends, thanks for all the love and support you have shown us, it has helped us more than any of you know. I love you all.

To all the staff in the Neonatal Unit at West Suffolk Hospital who looked after me when I needed it most - you are a credit to the hospital and your profession. To Dr. Evans for your positivity and for delivering that all important good news.

And to everyone who has helped me create this book. Gina for your friendship, advice and help getting word out about my book. Jon of Oleander Press for your knowledge and advice. Diane, Jan and Clare from West Suffolk Hospital and everyone at The Stroke Association. To Daddy and his design team at Coastline Graphics. Gareth for all your witchcraft creating the blog, James C and his brother for the ideas and to everyone who has contributed advice, proof reading, recipes and suggestions.

I hope you all enjoy the book, be sure to keep up to date with us at www.olivers-kitchen.co.uk

Ollie